rounds

Rounds is a series of circular characters whose real-life stories start where they end which is way they are called

rounds

Rounds is a series of circular characters whose real-life stories start where they end which is why they are called

To Lewis, with love

First published 2016 by Nosy Crow Ltd
The Crow's Nest, 10a Lant Street
London SE1 1QR
www.nosycrow.com

ISBN 978 0 85763 253 1 (HB)
ISBN 978 0 85763 558 7 (PB)

Nosy Crow and associated logos are trademarks
and/or registered trademarks of Nosy Crow Ltd.

Concept and story research by Barry Tranter and Emma Tranter
Text © Emma Tranter 2016
Illustrations © Barry Tranter 2016
Consultant: Chris Jarvis, Education Officer at the
Oxford University Museum of Natural History

A CIP catalogue record for this book is available from the British Library.

Printed in China by Imago

Papers used by Nosy Crow are made
from wood grown in sustainable forests.

1 3 5 7 9 8 6 4 2 (HB)
1 3 5 7 9 8 6 4 2 (PB)

Franklin Frog

Jump to it!

Barry Tranter

nosy crow

Emma Tranter

Meet Franklin. Franklin is a frog.
Here he is sitting on a lily pad in his pond.
Franklin loves being in and around water.

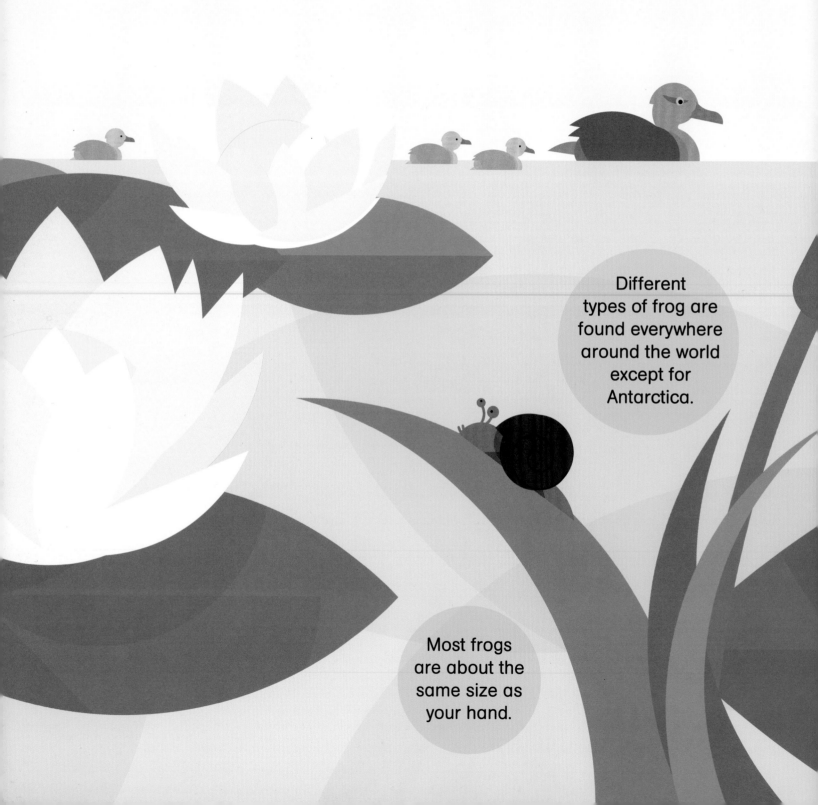

Different types of frog are found everywhere around the world except for Antarctica.

Most frogs are about the same size as your hand.

When Franklin is on land, he doesn't walk or crawl – he jumps instead. He can even cross the pond by jumping from one lily pad to the next.

Wheeeee!

Here I go!

Frogs use their strong back legs to jump.

Jumping is not the only way Franklin gets around – he swims too. His big, webbed feet push him through the water. It's a quick way to escape from danger. Look out for that heron, Franklin!

Frogs are eaten by lots of animals, including birds, badgers, otters and cats.

It's a great day for a swim!

Underwater, frogs breathe and drink through their skin.

Frogs can hide from herons underwater.

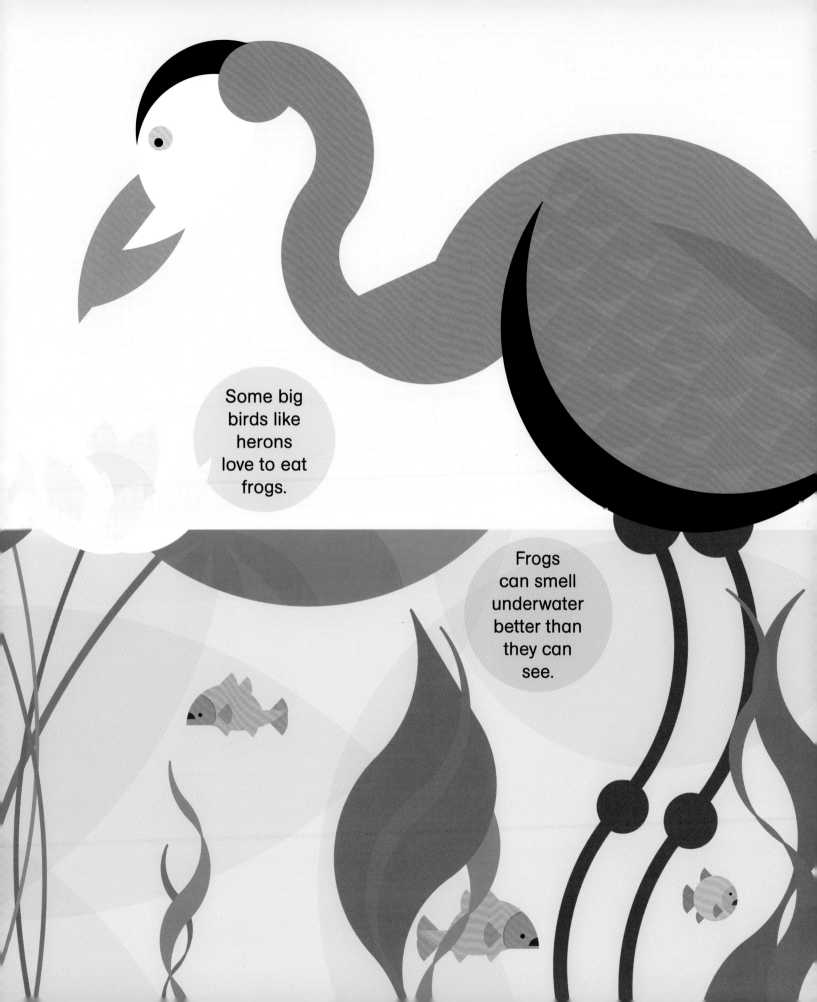

Some big birds like herons love to eat frogs.

Frogs can smell underwater better than they can see.

Franklin's feeling hungry now. He uses his long, sticky tongue to catch insects.

Mmmmm . . . juicy flies!

A frog's tongue coils up in its mouth, a bit like a party blower!

Adult frogs always eat on land, never in the water.

He's on the look-out for worms and snails, too!

Because frogs can't chew, they crush their food between their tongue and their eyeballs.

Frogs don't have necks, so they move their whole body in order to look around.

As the weather gets colder, Franklin must find a warm spot where he can hibernate for the winter. Hibernating is like having a long, deep sleep.

I'm off to bed. Now where shall I go?

Frogs often look for a pile of leaves to snuggle up in.

Because frogs can breathe underwater, some hibernate at the bottom of ponds.

Franklin sleeps through the short, dark days and long, cold nights of winter.

And as the snow falls,
he remains safely hidden.

In spring, the days grow warmer and Franklin wakes up. It's time to find a mate!

Hello, world!

But Franklin realises he's not the only frog looking for a mate! Lots of male frogs gather at night time and use special calls to attract females.

Frogs often return to the place where they were born to find a mate.

Frogs always meet in and around water to mate.

Some frogs' croaks can be heard up to one mile away!

Ready . . .

steady . . .

croak!

To croak, frogs fill up their throats with air, then push it out again.

At last, Franklin's call works. Here comes Felicity! She has travelled a very long way to be here.

Frogs start to mate when they are around two years old.

Hi there. I'm Franklin. What's your name?

During the mating season, frogs don't eat anything at all!

As spring arrives, Felicity lays hundreds of tiny eggs.

The frogs' eggs float near the surface of the water where the sun's warmth helps them grow.

Fish like to eat frogspawn. Frogs lay lots of eggs so that some will survive, even if most of them are eaten.

They are surrounded by a jelly which protects them. The eggs stick together in big clumps known as frogspawn.

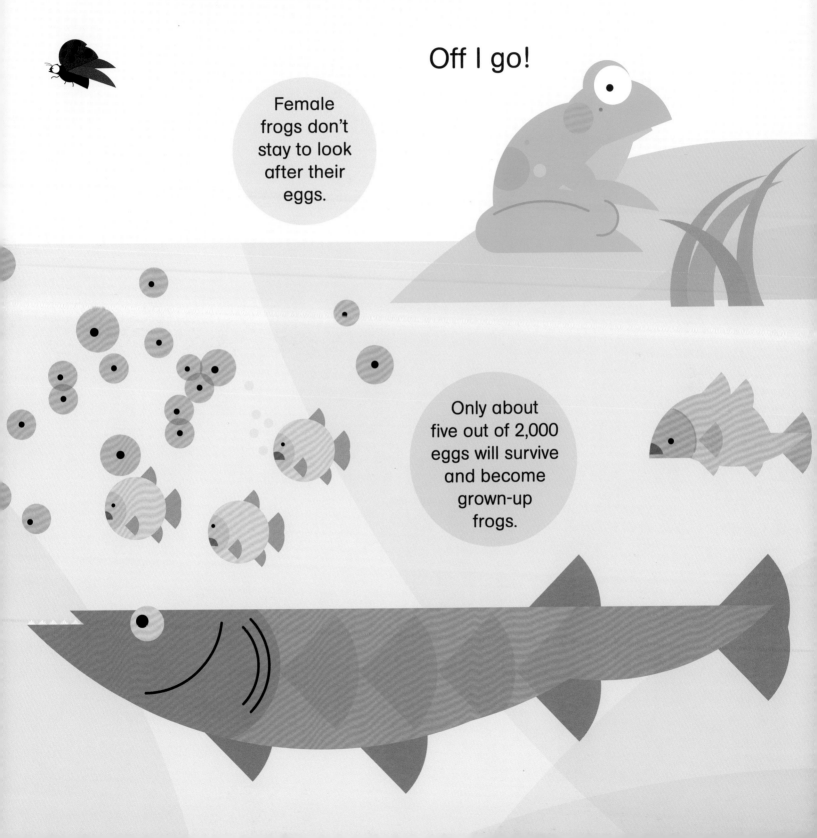

Off I go!

Female frogs don't stay to look after their eggs.

Only about five out of 2,000 eggs will survive and become grown-up frogs.

Inside each egg a tiny black creature forms. It is called a tadpole.

Tadpoles have gills, like fish, which means they can breathe in the water.

At first, tadpoles get food from inside their eggs.

Wow, I'm hatching!

After almost two weeks, the tadpole hatches and starts to swim around.

When they are four weeks old, tadpoles grow tiny teeth to grind their food.

I'm going to be a frog when I grow up!

Tadpoles mainly eat tiny plants called algae.

Throughout the spring,
the tadpole changes shape.

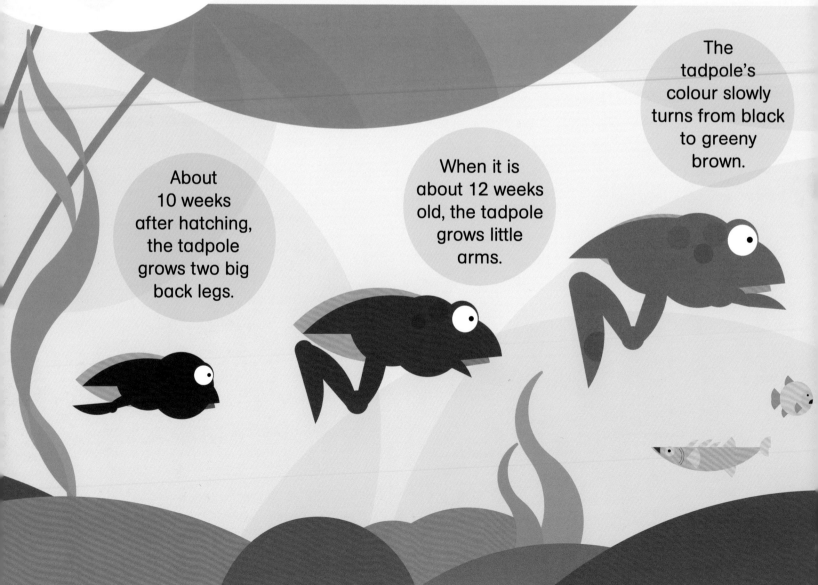

About
10 weeks
after hatching,
the tadpole
grows two big
back legs.

When it is
about 12 weeks
old, the tadpole
grows little
arms.

The
tadpole's
colour slowly
turns from black
to greeny
brown.

It slowly grows into a froglet,
and then into a frog.

Look – my tail
has disappeared.
I'm a frog!

At around
16 weeks old,
the grown-up
frog is ready
to leave the
pond.

After about
14 weeks, the
tadpole's tail
shrinks and it
becomes
a froglet.

Meet Fraser, Franklin's son. Fraser is a frog.
Here he is sitting on a lily pad in his pond.
Fraser loves being in and around water.

Hello, I'm Fraser.
Nice to meet you!

Frogs have been around for millions of years – since the time of the dinosaurs!

Most frogs live for about seven years.

The life cycle of a frog

rounds

Rounds is a series of circular characters whose real-life stories start where they end which is why they are called

Rounds is a series of circular characters whose real-life stories start where they end which is why they are called